SPACE SCIENCE

SCIENCE FOR EXPLORING SPACE

Mark Thompson

WAYLAND
www.waylandbooks.co.uk

First published in Great Britain in 2019 by Wayland
Copyright © Hodder and Stoughton, 2019
All rights reserved

Editor: Amy Pimperton
Design and illustration: Collaborate

HB ISBN: 978 1 5263 0845 0
PB ISBN: 978 1 5263 0846 7

Printed and bound in China

Wayland, an imprint of
Hachette Children's Group
Part of Hodder and Stoughton
Carmelite House
50 Victoria Embankment
London EC4Y 0DZ

An Hachette UK Company

www.hachette.co.uk
www.hachettechildrens.co.uk

The website addresses (URLs) included in this book were valid at the time of going to press. However, it is possible that contents or addresses may have changed since the publication of this book. No responsibility for any such changes can be accepted by either the author or the Publisher.

Picture credits: Every attempt has been made to clear copyright. Should there be any inadvertent omission please apply to the publisher for rectification.

Note: In the preparation of this book, all due care has been exercised with regard to the instructions, activities and techniques depicted. The publishers regret that they can accept no liability for any loss or injury sustained. Always get adult supervision and follow manufacturers' advice when using electric and battery-powered appliances.

CONTENTS

OUT OF THIS WORLD

Have you ever dreamed of travelling through space? Imagine seeing a planet, such as Saturn, through a telescope. You might be amazed to see a planet for real and wonder what it would be like to travel around the Universe, discovering amazing alien worlds.

People have stared in wonder at the night sky for thousands of years, but we have only been able to explore space for a few hundred years, mostly through the use of telescopes. If you could travel among the stars, what do you think you might you see there?

HELLO !

CHALLENGES

We have learned a lot through telescopes because it is very difficult for humans to travel and live in space. The distances are vast, and we need complicated technology to protect us from radiation and to deal with the effects of zero gravity, among many other things. Yet the desire to rocket into space is still an ambition for the human race.

SPACE PIONEERS

The first robotic space mission to successfully explore another planet was the *Mariner 2* spacecraft, which visited Venus in 1962. Seven years later, in 1969, the first humans to set foot on another world were the Apollo 11 astronauts Neil Armstrong (1930–2012) and Edwin 'Buzz' Aldrin (1930–), who, along with Mike Collins (1930–) travelled to the Moon.

FAR AND WIDE

Since those first days of space exploration we have sent robotic spacecraft to every planet in the solar system, as well as many moons. We have even visited the distant dwarf planet, Pluto, when the *New Horizons* spacecraft flew by in 2015. The discoveries these spacecraft have made are truly awe-inspiring!

In this book you can explore space for yourself and some of the amazing things we might find there by taking part in some great activities. You will go meteorite hunting, erupt a volcano just like Olympus Mons on Mars, explore hurricanes on Jupiter and see how giant gas clouds form.

HUNT FOR METEORITES

If you are very lucky, you might see a shooting star – or meteor – flash across the night sky. Meteors look like bright stars, but they are actually space rocks falling to Earth. As they fall, they squeeze gas in Earth's atmosphere in front of them. This then causes the rock to get hot and glow. Many space rocks burn up completely, but any that land on Earth are called meteorites.

Meteorites have fallen to Earth for millions of years, but they are hard to find. They look very similar to ordinary rocks or stones. In this activity you will hunt for stones that might show signs of life and test your rock samples – just like robotic spacecraft do on alien planets – to see if they are meteorites.

YOU WILL NEED:

- a bag or box to collect the rocks and stones in
- a couple of glass bowls
- some white vinegar
- a magnet
- an old ceramic kitchen tile

1 Collect rocks to test from a park, your garden, a beach or near a river. Look for rocks that are yellow or light brown in colour.

2 Take your glass bowls outside. Place a rock inside a bowl.

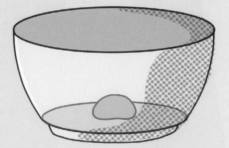

3 Pour white vinegar over the rock so that about half of the rock is covered. Wait, and watch what happens. If your rock fizzes and bubbles then it is limestone, which is a rock made of very old, dead creatures' bones and shells.

4 If your rock doesn't bubble, let it dry out. Hold a magnet close to it. If the magnet is attracted to the rock, then your rock has some metal inside it. This means that there is a chance it might be a meteorite!

5 If your rock does have metal in it, scrape it against the back of the kitchen tile. If the rock leaves a streak then it is probably just an ordinary rock.

If it leaves no streak then you may have found a meteorite! Take your rock along to your local museum or university to find out for sure.

Repeat steps 2 to 5 with your other rocks.

SPACE FACT

A rock named ALH84001 was found in 1984 on Antarctica. When scientists studied the rock they discovered tiny little gas bubbles trapped inside it that were exactly the same as the gas found in Mars' atmosphere. The rock had travelled all the way to Earth from Mars.

ERUPT A MARTIAN VOLCANO!

There are some amazing things in space – from comets whizzing around the solar system to diamond icebergs floating in the seas of Neptune. If you took a trip to Mars then you could see Olympus Mons – the largest volcano in the solar system. At 25 km high it makes even the largest of Earth's volcanoes look like rather small hills.

Olympus Mons is a shield volcano. Its gently sloping sides are made up from many layers of hardened lava. In this activity you will make 'lava' erupt with a chemical reaction!

YOU WILL NEED:

- a mixing bowl and spoon
- half a cup of flour
- half a cup of water
- a tablespoon of salt
- newspaper
- a clean, empty, small plastic drinks bottle
- a piece of cardboard about 30 cm x 30 cm
- some red-brown paint
- a paintbrush
- a sink or a large tray
- three teaspoons of bicarbonate of soda
- a piece of tissue paper
- a cup of white vinegar
- red food colouring
- washing-up liquid

1 Make papier-mâché glue by mixing the flour and water into a paste. Add the salt to stop it going mouldy. Tear up lots of strips of newspaper.

You are now ready to get messy and build your volcano.

2 Put the drinks bottle on the cardboard. Dip newspaper strips into the papier-mâché glue, then place them around the base of the bottle. Let them dry. Build up more layers around the bottle in a volcano shape. Leave a hole at the top.

When your volcano is completely dry, paint it a red-brown colour to match the rocks found on Mars. (Your volcano will be a different shape to Olympus Mons because of the bottle inside.)

3 When the paint is dry, put your volcano in a sink or on a tray. Wrap three teaspoons of bicarbonate of soda in a piece of tissue paper.

4 Pour the white vinegar into the bottle. Add a few drops of food colouring and a good squirt of washing-up liquid. Drop in your bicarbonate of soda and stand back. After a few seconds, red foamy lava should erupt out of your volcano!

SCIENCE FACT

The foam is a result of a chemical reaction between the acidic vinegar and the alkaline bicarbonate of soda. The reaction causes bubbles of carbon dioxide to be released, which are then trapped by the washing-up liquid.

SMASH INTO THE MOON

Look at the Moon without using a telescope and you might spot a few impact craters on the lunar surface. They are all caused by meteorites (see pages 6–7). When they smash into a moon (or planet) they make a dent, and the bigger the meteorite or the faster it is going, the bigger the dent!

Look at the Moon through a telescope and you will see lots more impact craters. In this fun, but rather messy activity, you can create impact craters with your own meteorites, just like those on the Moon.

YOU WILL NEED:

- a tray with deep sides
- newspaper
- flour
- a sieve
- a spoon
- cocoa powder
- modelling clay
- a ruler
- a notebook and pencil

1 Put the tray on some newspaper. Fill it about 5 cm deep with flour. Try to get it level and without any lumps or bumps in it.

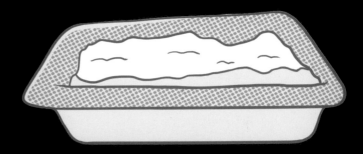

2 Use a sieve and spoon to sprinkle the cocoa powder on top of the flour to form a thick layer. This is your lunar surface.

3 Make a number of different-sized balls with the modelling clay. These are your meteorites.

4 Hold one of the balls about 1 m above the tray and drop it.

Carefully take it out without disturbing the crater. Notice how the cocoa powder is now covered with flour from inside the crater. Measure and note down how far from the hole the flour has spread.

MAXIMUM IMPACT!

Try it again with different-sized balls and from different heights. Does it make any difference to the size of the crater? How big is the biggest impact crater you can make?

What do you think happens on the Moon when meteorites of different sizes hit the surface or if they travel at different speeds?

SCIENCE FACT

The Moon isn't the only place where you can find impact craters. All the planets have them and there are about 190 known meteorite craters on Earth. Scientists think that a large meteorite, about 10–15 km wide, hit the Earth 66 million years ago. It created a giant crater about 180 km across in Mexico. The result of the impact is thought to have killed off the dinosaurs.

'TALK' LIKE A COMPUTER

Astronauts talking to mission control, or a mission controller sending important commands to a robotic spacecraft, have to communicate across thousands or even millions of kilometres. This is usually done with radio dishes, which look like large television satellite dishes. The communication is sent by translating words or commands into a long sequence of ones and zeros.

The ones and zeros are known as the binary alphabet. Each letter has a unique sequence of eight numbers. For example, the letter 'A' is written as 01000001. In this activity you will translate messages into binary and back again.

YOU WILL NEED:

- a pen
- a piece of paper
- a friend or family member to help you

1 If you were on a spacecraft, think of a question you would want to ask your friend or family member, such as "How is my cat?".

2 Look at the binary code alphabet on page 13. Write down on a piece of paper each letter in your sentence in its binary code.

Binary messages show the ones and zeros are in one long string. Each letter is a group of eight numbers, so when you write your message don't put in any spaces. For example, the word 'NO' would be written as 0100111001001111.

HELLO !

BINARY CODE

A 01000001	**G** 01000111	**M** 01001101	**T** 01010100
B 01000010	**H** 01001000	**N** 01001110	**U** 01010101
C 01000011	**I** 01001001	**O** 01001111	**V** 01010110
D 01000100	**J** 01001010	**P** 01010000	**W** 01010111
E 01000101	**K** 01001011	**Q** 01010001	**X** 01011000
F 01000110	**L** 01001100	**R** 01010010	**Y** 01011001
		S 01010011	**Z** 01011010

3 Give the message to your helper with the code above. Ask them to translate the message, and then read it out to see if they have translated it correctly.

4 Ask them to reply in code. Translate it to find the answer.

SPACE FACT

Communicating in space is hard because the distances between things are so great. If you were on the Moon it would take just over a second for your message to travel the 384,400 km to reach Earth. If you were on Pluto, it would take five hours for your message to travel the 7.5 billion km between Earth and this distant dwarf planet.

FREEZE A COMET

Comets are space objects made of rock, dust, ice and other frozen chemicals, such as ammonia. They are known as 'dirty snowballs', and are a bit like a big handful of snow with stones or soil mixed in with it.

Comets are normally found at the edge of the solar system. Occasionally their orbits bring them close to the Sun, where they warm up. This causes some of the comet's ice to turn into a gas (this is called sublimation). The 'tail' of the comet is great jets of gas streaming behind it. In this activity you will make a small comet with a gas tail.

YOU WILL NEED:

- safety goggles and gloves (you must wear these during the WHOLE activity)
- a black bin bag
- a bowl
- half a jug of cold water
- quarter of a jug of soil
- smelling salts or ammonia (ask an adult to buy the smelling salts from a chemists. If they can't get smelling salts, then ammonia from a hardware store is just as good.)
- soy sauce
- dry ice (ask an adult to buy this from an online supplier)
- a tea towel
- a hammer

1 Put on the safety goggles and gloves. Put the black bin bag inside the bowl. Pour in the cold water and the soil. This represents the water and rock found in comets.

RED ALERT!

Ask an adult to help you when using the hammer and when handling soil, dry ice, ammonia or smelling salts.

2 Next, add either a heaped teaspoon of smelling salts or a good squirt of ammonia. This stuff is really smelly, so DO NOT get too close. There are organic materials on comets, so add some soy sauce to represent this.

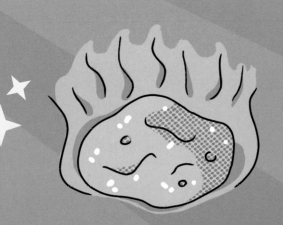

3 Tip a full jug of dry ice on to the tea towel. Fold the towel over so that no ice escapes.

With the hammer, break the ice into small pieces, then tip all of it into the bin bag. When dry ice mixes with water, it turns from a solid to a gas.

4 With you hands outside the bag, squeeze the contents together. It should take less than a minute and quite a bit of squeezing, but you will feel when it is a solid lump of ice.

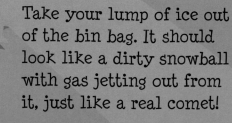

5 Take your lump of ice out of the bin bag. It should look like a dirty snowball with gas jetting out from it, just like a real comet!

SPACE FACT

Comets take many years to orbit the Sun. Halley's Comet is a famous comet that takes around 76 years to orbit the Sun once. It is due back in our sky again in 2061!

CREATE GRAVITY ...IN A BUCKET!

In space, big objects, such as the Sun and the planets, pull smaller objects towards them. Their large size makes a strong gravitational pull.

In space you will float around in a spacecraft unless you can create your own gravity. This is because you and the spacecraft are all free-falling at the same speed towards a bigger object, such as Earth, due to its large gravitational pull.

One way to create gravity is through acceleration, which is when something starts to go faster or if it changes direction. You may have felt the effect of acceleration in a lift. When a lift starts to accelerate upwards, notice how you feel a little bit heavier. You can use acceleration to create your own force of gravity in a bucket!

YOU WILL NEED:
- waterproof clothing (optional)
- a bucket
- some water

1 If you want to, put on your waterproof clothing. Fill the bucket about two-thirds full of cold water.

Take the bucket outside and turn it upside down! Gravity pulls the water out of the bucket and you get a wet floor and possibly wet feet!

RED ALERT!
Do this activity outside in a clear, open space!

2 Fill the bucket again, about two-thirds full of water. Go outside and this time make sure no one nor anything breakable is near you, just in case the handle breaks or you let go!

Swing the bucket from side to side, gradually swinging higher and higher.

3 When you are ready, and in one smooth movement, swing the bucket over your head in a circle. If you feel confident, keep this going for a few loops. The water doesn't fall out because the acceleration of the bucket pins the water inside it, simulating gravity.

4 You might think you are now stuck with a bucket of cold water swinging around your head! You can stop it by going back to the large swinging motions when the bucket is near the ground. Gradually reduce the swing and you shouldn't get wet.

SCIENCE FACT

If your bedroom was in space and you could spin it around about 17 times per minute, then it would feel like gravity was pulling you to the ceiling and you could sit up there and read this book!

BEND WATER ... WITH A COMB!

Beyond the solar system and out among the stars are some really amazing sights, such as black holes or huge glowing clouds of gas and dust, called nebulae. About 5 billion years ago, the solar system formed out of a nebula. You can see nebulae from Earth – see if you can spot the Orion Nebula in the night sky.

Before a nebula can turn into planets or stars, something must make the gas and dust clump together. An electrostatic force can do this. When big enough clumps have formed, gravity does the rest and stars and planets form. A comb can help you see an electrostatic force in action!

YOU WILL NEED:

- tissue paper
- a plastic comb
- a sink with a cold water tap
- a towel

1 Rip up the tissue paper and roll it into about twenty pea-sized balls.

2 Put your comb close to the pieces of paper and ... nothing will happen. Neither the comb nor the pieces of paper have an electrostatic charge.

SCIENCE FACT

Magnets have a north pole and a south pole. The north pole of one magnet repels the north poll of another, but is attracted to the other magnet's south pole. All matter, such as dust, is made of atoms. Inside an atom are positively charged protons and negatively charged electrons. Just like a magnet's poles, two positives or two negatives push apart, but a positive *and* a negative attract. This attraction is what causes space dust to clump together.

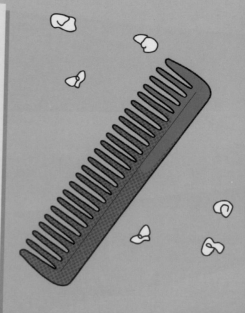

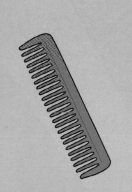

3 Turn on the cold tap so you have a thin, steady flow of water. Put the comb near to it and ... the stream of water should not change.

4 Dry the comb on the towel. Run the comb through your hair a few times. This will give the comb a negative electrostatic charge.

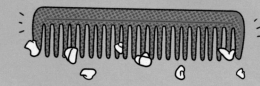

5 Put the comb close to the tissue paper again. The comb's negative charge causes the tissue paper to become positively charged and attracted to the comb.

6 Comb your hair again and then put the comb close to the stream of water. The flow of water has a positive charge, so it should bend a little as it is attracted to the comb.

SCIENCE FACT

Electrostatic force is used in a type of rocket engine known as an ion drive. Xenon gas is pumped into the engine and the gas's atoms are attracted to the back of the engine by an electrostatic force. They are then pushed out to push the rocket forwards.

EXPLORE VENUS'S ATMOSPHERE

Venus is the second planet from the Sun, but it is the hottest planet in the solar system, with a temperature of 462 °C! This is because Venus has a very thick atmosphere, which is the name for the gases that surround a planet.

The gases around Venus trap heat, like a greenhouse, so they are called greenhouse gases. The main gas that surrounds Venus is carbon dioxide. It is the same gas that we breathe out and it is also made by burning fossil fuels, such as coal. In this activity you will see what happens when we use a material to create a greenhouse effect and trap heat inside a container.

YOU WILL NEED:

- an adult to help you as this activity might get a bit hot
- a glass bowl
- some dark paper or cloth
- a small cup that can sit inside the bowl
- a thermometer
- a notebook and pen
- cling film

1 On a sunny day, line the glass bowl with the dark paper or dark cloth.

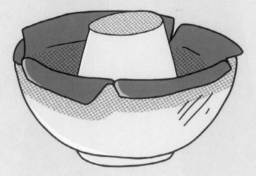

2 Place the small cup upside down in the centre of the bowl.

3 Balance the thermometer carefully on top of the cup and leave it on a windowsill in full sun for an hour. Note down the temperature on the thermometer.

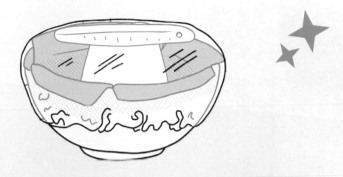

4 Stretch some cling film across the top of the bowl so that the thermometer is trapped inside.

5 Place the bowl on a windowsill and leave it in full sun again for an hour.

The cling film should trap the heat from the Sun and create an artificial atmosphere. The reading on the thermometer should show a higher temperature. Ask an adult to help you with this, just in case the bowl is hot.

SPACE FACT

Venus really is a horrible place to go on holiday. The atmosphere of Venus makes it impossible for us to survive on the surface and the temperature is far too hot. It also rains sulphuric acid, which would dissolve the skin off your body!

MAKE A FRUIT SOLAR SYSTEM

It can be difficult to understand how big the stars and planets really are. From Earth they all look like small spots of light in the sky. Earth seems big to us because we are so close to it. The Sun is so big that you could fit about one million Earth's inside it!

It is impossible to make a real-sized model of the solar system's planets. It would be too big and too heavy! Space scientists make scale models to compare sizes. You can make a model that is about 400 million times smaller in scale ... from fruit!

YOU WILL NEED:

- a pen and paper
- a calculator
- a ruler
- a knife and chopping board
- the following pieces of fruit:
  a blueberry, a large olive, two cherry tomatoes, two grapefruit, a large melon and a watermelon

RED ALERT!

Ask an adult to help you use the knife.

1 Copy the table below on to a piece of paper.

Planet	Planet diameter in km	Planet diameter in cm	Planet scaled size in cm (scale 423,687,000)	Which fruit?
Mercury	4,879			
Venus	12,104			
Earth	12,742			
Mars	6,779			
Jupiter	139,822			
Saturn	116,464			
Uranus	50,724			
Neptune	49,244			

* table answers on page 32

2 Convert each planet diameter to centimetres by multiplying each number in kilometres by 100,000. Write the answers in your table.

3 To work out which piece of fruit represents each planet, you need to scale down the size of the planets.

The fruits are about 423 million times smaller than the planets. Divide the diameter of each planet in centimetres by 423,687,000 (this number is called a scaling factor). Write down the answers in the table.

4 Ask an adult to help you cut each fruit in half. Measure the diameter of each piece of fruit. Compare the fruit diameter in cm to the scaled diameter of the planets.

5 Match each planet with a piece of fruit. Line them up in the correct order to create a scale model of the solar system's planets.

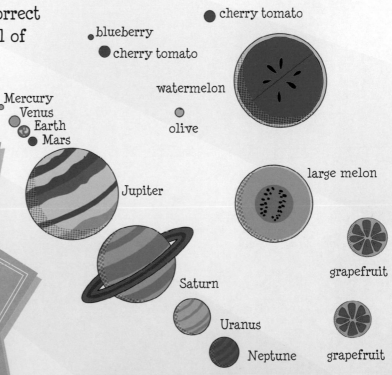

cherry tomato

blueberry

cherry tomato

watermelon

Mercury
Venus
Earth
Mars

olive

large melon

Jupiter

grapefruit

Saturn

Uranus

Neptune

grapefruit

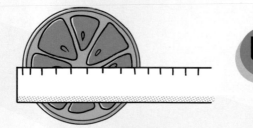

WHIP UP A STORM ... IN A BOTTLE

The Sun warms Earth, which then reflects heat to warm the gases in the atmosphere. Warm gas rises and cooler gas falls. This creates movement that we feel as wind or even as cyclones and hurricanes.

All the solar system's planets – except Mercury – have an atmosphere and some sort of weather. Jupiter's atmosphere contains hundreds of storms, including a massive hurricane called the Great Red Spot. It is just like the hurricanes we have on Earth but a LOT bigger. In this activity you can make your own Jupiter-style hurricane in a bottle!

YOU WILL NEED:

- two clean, dry, empty 2 litre plastic drinks bottles with the labels removed
- some water
- food colouring
- PVA glue
- gaffer tape

1 Fill one bottle about three-quarters full of water. Add a few drops of food colouring.

2 Put some PVA glue around the top of the neck. Place the neck of the second bottle on top of the glue to join the necks together. When the glue is dry put some more glue around the join. Let this dry, too.

3 To make the join extra-secure, wind some gaffer tape tightly around it.

4 Now you are ready to make a Great Red Spot hurricane! Grasp the join between the two bottles in one hand, flip the bottles over so the water filled bottle is upside down, and quickly move your hand around in tiny circles. This will cause the 'atmosphere' (the water) in the bottle to rotate, just like the gases in a hurricane do.

A 'tornado' will form as the vortex of water descends into the bottom bottle and air rises into the top bottle.

VORTEX

A vortex is the name for a spinning mass of fluid or air. Flip the bottle over and spin the bottle again. This time look down into the bottle from above to see the vortex created by the spinning 'atmosphere'.

SPACE FACT

The winds on Neptune are the fastest in the solar system. They can reach speeds of 2,200 kilometres per hour (km/h). That's almost supersonic – almost as fast as the speed of sound!

FIND THE SPEED of LIGHT ...WITH CHEESE!

The visible light we can see is one small part of the electromagnetic spectrum. Invisible parts of the electromagnetic spectrum include infrared, gamma rays, X-rays, radio waves and microwaves.

All parts of the spectrum travel at the speed of light: 299,792,458 metres per second (m/s). To work out this speed you need to know the light's wavelength and its frequency. Think of waves on the sea; wavelength is the distance between the top of two waves and frequency is how many waves pass you per second. Investigate the speed of microwaves – and the speed of light – with cheese!

YOU WILL NEED:

- a slice of bread
- some cheese (pre-sliced cheese works best for this activity)
- a microwave oven
- a microwavable bowl
- a microwavable plate
- a ruler

RED ALERT!

Ask an adult to help you use the microwave. NEVER put anything metallic in a microwave.

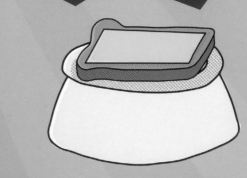

1 Neatly cover a slice of bread with cheese.

2 If your microwave oven has a rotating plate, remove it. Place the bowl over the spinning bit in the middle. Put the bread and cheese on the plate and on top of the bowl. This stops the bread and cheese from rotating.

3 Heat the bread and cheese on low power for about 30 seconds or until you see some melted lines in the cheese.

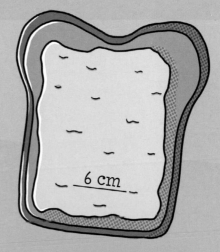

6 cm

4 Measure the distances between the lines in cm. The distances should all be the same, because the microwaves only warm the cheese in certain places. To find the wavelength of the microwave oven, multiply one of the measurements by two and then divide by 100.

2.45 GHz

5 Look for a sticker on the oven with the frequency on it. If it is in GHz, then multiply that number by 1,000,000,000. If it is in MHz then multiply that number by 1,000,000.

6 Finally multiply together the numbers from steps 4 and 5. This will give you the speed of light. How close did you get to 299,792,458 m/s?

SCIENCE FACT
The speed of light was first calculated in 1676 by a Danish astronomer called Ole Rømer (1644–1710). He was studying the moons of Jupiter and made very accurate timings of the eclipses he saw when the moons passed behind the planet.

SUPERCOOL WATER!

You might think that the only place you will find water in the solar system is here on Earth. Surprisingly, there is water out in space, and much closer than you might think. The Moon, comets and many other planets and moons have water, mainly in the form of ice.

You wouldn't expect to find running water on Mars, because it's surface temperature is so cold (on average -55 °C). But scientists have found evidence of salty water flowing on the surface. If water has salt (a mineral) in it, then it can be supercooled. This means it stays liquid at a lower temperature than ordinary water. In this activity, you can make supercooled water.

YOU WILL NEED:

- a 500 ml bottle of still mineral water
- a freezer
- an ice cube
- a plate

1 Leave a bottle of still mineral water to stand for a few minutes, somewhere that it will not get knocked or disturbed.

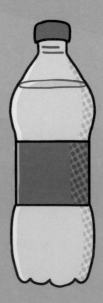

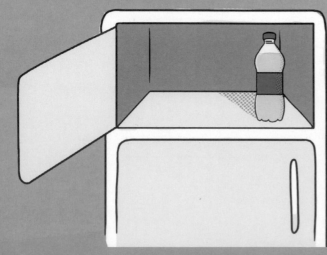

2 Place the mineral water carefully in a freezer.

3 Leave the bottle of water in the freezer for an hour. Make sure it doesn't get knocked.

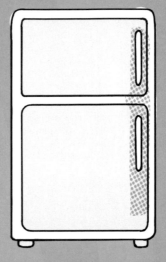

4 After an hour, carefully take the bottle out of the freezer. It should be very cold, but not frozen. If it is frozen, then try again with a second bottle for a shorter amount of time.

5 Put an ice cube on a plate. Pour a little water from your bottle on to the ice cube. If the water is supercooled then you will see a tiny tower of ice start to form. The ice cube gives the ice crystals something to form on.

Mineral water can be supercooled because it has minerals, such as salts or calcium, in it and it does not have any impurities in it.

SPACE FACT

It is thought by many scientists that the water on Earth came from comets smashing on to the surface.

GLOSSARY

ACCELERATION a change in speed or direction of a moving object

ATMOSPHERE the gases that surround a planet

BINARY a code used in communication, often between computers where everything is a group of ones and zeros

BLACK HOLE the dead core of a star

COMET a space object made of rock and ice that orbits the Sun

CRATER the dent in a planet or moon's surface, caused by an object crashing into it

CYCLONE a rapidly rotating wind system

ECLIPSE when astronomical objects line up and cause light from one to be blocked by another

FOSSIL FUEL fuel formed from the remains of living things

FREQUENCY the number of waves per second from light or other forms of radiation

GAS one of the three main states of matter. A gas can expand, squeeze, and flow from one place to another.

GRAVITY a force that tries to pull two objects together

HURRICANE a storm with very strong winds

LAVA hot, molten rock that has erupted from a volcano

MATTER stuff that makes up everything around us and is usually either a solid, a liquid or a gas

METEOR a space rock that emits light as it burns in the atmosphere

METEORITE a space rock that has landed on Earth or another planet

MOON a planet's natural satellite

ORBIT a circular or oval path one object follows around another

ORGANIC made from living things

RADIATION waves of energy, some of which can make people ill

SIMULATE to imitate the appearance or characteristics of something

SOLAR SYSTEM the planets, moons and other space objects that orbit the Sun

SPEED OF LIGHT maximum possible speed of any matter, which is 299,792,458 m/s

SUBLIMATION the process where solid objects turn into a gas, without turning into a liquid first

SUPERCOOLED a liquid that is below its freezing temperature, but is still liquid

VOLCANO a mountain with a crater or vent from which molten rock and hot gas erupts

WAVELENGTH the distance between two peaks in a sound or light wave

FURTHER INFORMATION

BOOKS

A Guide to Space by Kevin Pettman (Wayland, 2019)

Infographic Top Ten: Record-Breaking Earth & Space by Jon Richards and Ed Simkins (Wayland, 2016)

Science in a Flash: Earth and Space by Georgia Amson-Bradshaw (Franklin Watts, 2018)

Straightforward with Science: The Earth in Space by Peter Riley (Franklin Watts, 2018)

Planet Earth: Journey into Space by Michael Bright (Wayland, 2016)

HELLO !

PLACES TO VISIT

National Space Centre, Leicester
Science Museum, London
Glasgow Science Centre, Glasgow
Winchester Science Centre, Winchester

WEBSITES

The NASA Kids website has loads of interactive space activities, such as building your own rocket and trying your hand at driving a Martian buggy.
www.nasa.gov/kidsclub/index.html

National Geographic Kids is a great website with loads of curriculum-based science activities.
www.natgeokids.com/uk/category/discover/science/

The ESA Kids website has plenty of fun and games for kids to explore space.
www.esa.int/esaKIDSen/

INDEX

Planet	Planet diameter in km	Planet diameter in cm	Planet scaled size in cm (scale 423,687,000)	Which fruit?
Mercury	4,879	487,900,000	1.2	blueberry
Venus	12,104	1,210,400,000	2.9	cherry tomato
Earth	12,742	1,274,200,000	3	cherry tomato
Mars	6,779	677,900,000	1.6	olive
Jupiter	139,822	13,982,200,000	33	watermelon
Saturn	116,464	11,646,400,000	27.5	melon
Uranus	50,724	5,072,400,000	12	grapefruit
Neptune	49,244	4,924,400,000	11.5	grapefruit

* answers to the calculations on pages 22-23

SPACE SCIENCE

TITLES IN THIS SERIES

Born in Norfolk, author **MARK THOMPSON** has had a fascination with all things in the sky ever since he was a small boy. At the age of 10 he got his first view through a telescope; Saturn in all its glory. It ignited a passion that has stayed with him ever since.

Mark has inspired millions of viewers to get out and enjoy the night sky through his role as presenter on the RTS nominated show *BBC Stargazing Live*. His passion for reaching out to a new audience has found him working on *The One Show*, *This Morning*, Channel 4 documentaries and ITV's prime time breakfast show, *Good Morning*. He is also a regular face on *BBC Breakfast*, *Five News* and a regular voice on *Radio Five Live*.

SCIENCE FOR EXPLORING OUTER SPACE

Out of This World
Hunt for Meteorites
Erupt a Martian Volcano!
Smash into the Moon
'Talk' like a Computer
Freeze a Comet
Create Gravity ... in a Bucket!

Bend Water ... with a Comb
Explore Venus's Atmosphere
Make a Fruit Solar System
Whip Up a Storm ... in a Bottle
Find the Speed of Light ... with Cheese!
Supercool Water

SCIENCE FOR LOOKING INTO SPACE

Staring into Space
Measure the Moon
See Where the Sun ... Sets
Observe Earth's Spin
Tell the Time ... with Shadows
Build a Telescope
Observe the Sun

Become the Lunar Phases
Hunt for Alien Worlds
See Colours ... with a Spectroscope
Explore the Doppler Effect
Capture Star Trails
Build an Astrolabe

SCIENCE FOR ROCKETING INTO SPACE

Reach for the Stars
Escape Gravity
Overcome Inertia ... with an egg
Explore Epic Exothermic Eruptions
Balloon to the Moon
Lower the Centre of Gravity
Blast Off ... with a Chemical Reaction

Launch a Straw Rocket ... with Puff Power
Hurtle to Earth on an 'Eggciting' Mission
Send a Rocket into Orbit
Make Water Weightless
Become a Rocket Booster
Launch the Ultimate Rocket!

SCIENCE FOR SURVIVING IN SPACE

A Dangerous Place
Pack a Space Bag
Inflate a Balloon ... with Microbes
Eat Like an Astronaut
Warm Up with Insulation
Shield Yourself from Meteoroids
Grow Food in Space

Draw a Magnetic Force Field
Make a Biosphere ... in a Jar!
Make Dirty Water Clean (ish!)
Make Your Own Blood
Create Floating Blobs of Water
Cook Toast in a Solar Oven

www.markthompsonastronomy.com   www.spectacularscienceshow.com